FOREWORD

Accidents have occurred in the ECE region resulting in adverse impacts on inland waters and aquatic ecosystems which often extend beyond the country of origin. The emergency situations which developed have in many cases revealed a degree of unpreparedness at both national and international levels. Their occurrence has underscored gaps in existing legislation or lack of measures and procedures to cope efficiently with emergencies and their transboundary environmental impacts.

The adoption of the Code of Conduct by the Economic Commission for Europe in 1990 represents the first collective response by ECE member Governments to the need to reinforce international co-operation in preventing and combating accidental pollution. The Code was elaborated by the Senior Advisers to ECE Governments on Environmental and Water Problems through its Working Party on Water Problems, with the financial support of UNEP.

In adopting the *Code of Conduct on Accidental Pollution of Transboundary Inland Waters*, the Commission recommended that Governments apply the Code of Conduct as an essential element of further co-operation among them and as an input to national water pollution control policies. Furthermore, the Commission invited member Governments to develop or strengthen methodologies, measures and practices regarding the accidental pollution of transboundary inland waters, both at the pre-accident and post-accident stages.

In the light of the outcome of the CSCE Meeting on the Protection of the Environment held in Sofia (Bulgaria) in 1989, the Senior Advisers to ECE Governments on Environmental and Water Problems are undertaking, with the assistance of the *Ad Hoc* Working Group, the elaboration of a convention on the transboundary impacts of industrial accidents. The preparation of this document will be based on, *inter alia*, the relevant provisions of the *Code of Conduct on Accidental Pollution of Transboundary Inland Waters*.

Contents

ECONOMIC COMMISSION FOR EUROPE
Geneva

CODE OF CONDUCT
on
Accidental Pollution of
Transboundary Inland Waters

*as adopted by the Economic Commission for Europe
at its forty-fifth session (1990)
by decision C(45)*

*The Code of Conduct was prepared under the auspices
of the Senior Advisers to ECE Governments
on Environmental and Water Problems
and funded under ECE/UNEP Project FP/5201-87-04*

UNITED NATIONS
New York, 1990

NOTE

The designations employed and the presentation of the material in this publication do not imply the expression of any opinion whatsoever on the part of the Secretariat of the United Nations concerning the legal status of any country, territory, city or area, or of its authorities, or concerning the delimitation of its frontiers or boundaries.

E/ECE/1225
ECE/ENVWA/16

UNITED NATIONS PUBLICATION
Sales No. E.90.II.E.28
ISBN 92-1-116485-0

01000P

INTRODUCTION

1.   This Code is intended to guide Governments in the protection of transboundary inland waters against pollution resulting from hazardous activities in case of accidents or natural disasters and in mitigating their impacts on the aquatic environment. It deals, in particular, with the transboundary effects of such pollution. It is aimed at the harmonization of national measures to be taken in this field and at the formulation of basic frames of international co-operation.

2.   The Code lays down those measures which countries concerned should take individually or jointly to prevent, control and reduce accidental pollution of transboundary inland waters. Its objective is also to increase the state of preparedness to respond efficiently to such incidents, to mitigate and contain the damage resulting therefrom, to provide a common basis for, and establish standards of, conduct relating to hazardous activities that might affect transboundary inland waters.

3.   One of the basic functions of the Code is to serve as a point of reference, particularly until such time as countries have entered into relevant bilateral or multilateral agreements.

4.   The Code is without prejudice to the provisions of particular systems or procedures included in national legislation or in bilateral or multilateral instruments concluded for this purpose. Countries should endeavour to apply and further develop the objectives of the Code either within the framework of existing international agreements or through the elaboration and adoption of new agreements as appropriate, taking into account the relevant work of competent international bodies in this field.

5.   The Code does not preclude countries from instituting more stringent national regulations as well as broader and more frequent co-operative measures with other countries concerned.

6.   The Code applies to hazardous activities which result in or are likely to result in accidental pollution of transboundary inland waters in the territory of other countries, especially that resulting from:

- The extraction, production, processing or movement of hazardous substances;

- The unintended release of hazardous substances in the form of gases, liquids, or solids into water bodies;

- The surface or underground storage of hazardous substances;

- The misuse of hazardous substances and/or of technologies;

- Natural disasters.

Inasmuch as matters regarding the transport of dangerous goods including hazardous substances and wastes, as well as those regarding radioactive substances, are covered by relevant existing international instruments, these are not referred to in the Code.

7.   The Code applies to any incident irrespective of whether it occurred in the transboundary inland waters or in their vicinity with the risk of affecting such waters.

8.   This Code should be brought to the attention of all concerned with the utilization and protection of transboundary inland waters so that Governments assume their shared responsibility, individually or jointly, to ensure that the objectives of the Code are met.

I. DEFINITIONS

For the purposes of this Code:

(a) **"Incident"** means any man-made accident or natural disaster;

(b) **"Accidental pollution of transboundary inland waters"** means the introduction, directly or indirectly, of hazardous substances into transboundary inland waters as a result of incidents originating wholly or partly within an area under the jurisdiction of one country, which causes or threatens to cause significant impairment of the quality of transboundary inland waters and/or significant damage to aquatic ecosystems in an area under the jurisdiction of another country;

(c) **"Transboundary inland waters"** means any surface and ground waters which form or cross the common boundaries of two or more countries;

(d) **"Accident"** means a departure from normally permissible operating conditions of an activity causing or threatening to cause water pollution;

(e) **"Natural disaster"** means any natural event including such phenomena as floods, ice drifts, earthquakes, landslides and hurricanes, which causes or threatens to cause accidental pollution of transboundary inland waters;

(f) **"Risk"** means the combined effect of the probability of occurrence of an undesirable event and its magnitude;

(g) **"Hazardous activity"** means any activity which by its nature involves a significant risk of accidental pollution of transboundary inland waters;

(h) **"Hazardous substance"** means any substance or energy involving a significant risk of accidental pollution of transboundary inland waters, including toxic, persistent and bio-accumulative substances and harmful micro-organisms;

(i) **"Riparian country"** means any country bordering on a given transboundary inland water;

3

(j) **"Country concerned"** means any country of incident and any exposed country;

(k) **"Country of incident"** means any country within the territory and under the jurisdiction of which accidental pollution of transboundary inland waters originates or is likely to originate;

(l) **"Exposed country"** means any country affected by, or exposed to a significant risk of, accidental pollution of transboundary inland waters;

(m) **"Authorizing country"** means any country authorizing hazardous activities or activities involving hazardous substances;

(n) **"Operator"** means any physical or legal person planning to carry out, or carrying out, a hazardous activity, such as manufacturing, processing, storing, disposing, distributing, transporting, handling, discharging, recovering or consuming hazardous substances.

II. GENERAL PROVISIONS

1. Countries should in particular take, and adapt to circumstances, strict measures relating to hazardous activities and substances according to safety standards using the best available technology to prevent, control and reduce accidental pollution of transboundary inland waters and minimize the risk of damage, and/or to mitigate and contain the damage from such pollution.

2. In taking measures to control and regulate hazardous activities and substances, to prevent and control accidental pollution, to mitigate damage arising from accidental pollution, countries should do everything so as not to transfer, directly or indirectly, damage or risks between different environmental media or transform one type of pollution into another.

3. Riparian countries should implement, within the framework of their national legislation, the basic principle that responsibility for pollution lies with the polluter.

4.   In the interest of rational management of transboundary inland waters and their protection against accidental pollution, riparian countries are called upon to use the provisions of this Code including the annexes hereto, as guidance to enhance co-operation in this field.

III.   NATIONAL LEGISLATIVE AND ADMINISTRATIVE MEASURES

1.   Countries should take appropriate legislative and administrative measures for the prevention, control and reduction of accidental pollution of transboundary inland waters and for the mitigation and containment of damage resulting therefrom. Such measures should cover the matters referred to in annex A, and particular attention should be given to hazardous substances, especially those which are toxic, persistent and bio-accumulative.

2.   National legislative and administrative measures should promote the development and sound application of the best available technologies and their safe operation for efficient prevention, control and reduction of accidental pollution of transboundary inland waters.   These measures should also provide for the competent authorities to be authorized to take emergency action without delay.

IV.   INTERNATIONAL CO-OPERATION

1.   Countries should make use of existing bilateral or multilateral agreements and institutional arrangements to cope with accidental pollution of transboundary inland waters and should, where necessary, expand their scope and functions to cover matters governed by this Code including the annexes hereto.

2.   Riparian countries should, in the framework of bilateral or mutilateral agreements or arrangements, define their mutual relations regarding the control of hazardous activities and the prevention of accidental pollution of transboundary inland waters, in order to ensure mutually agreed regulation of their conduct.

3. Bilateral and multilateral agreements or arrangements should contain, in particular, provisions on appropriate mutual exchange of all pertinent information, early warning and alarm systems, joint contingency plans, preventive and remedial measures, institutional infrastructures and joint manoeuvres and exercises of competent services, such as civil protection, rescue units, fire and oil brigades, common procedures concerning risk assessment and environmental impact assessment as well as those relating to responsibility and liability, and measures to remedy damage caused by accidental pollution of transboundary inland waters. Agreements or arrangements in this framework should provide for the necessary international institutions to ensure implementation.

4. Riparian countries should agree to co-ordinate and harmonize as necessary their legislative and administrative measures relating to transboundary inland waters, particularly as regards criteria for defining hazardous activities and substances, contingency plans at all levels, monitoring, safety and other relevant matters.

5. When a country of incident receives information from another riparian country that activities envisaged or carried out in the territory of the country of incident are likely to cause accidental pollution of transboundary inland waters in the territory of the other country, both countries should without undue delay commence consultations and negotiations as appropriate aimed at achieving mutually acceptable solutions.

V. INSTITUTIONAL ARRANGEMENTS

1. International institutions for transboundary inland waters should, where appropriate, be entrusted with the functions specified in annex B.

2. Where commissions or other institutional arrangements are already set up, participating countries should make full use of them by providing all necessary means for the efficient implementation of their tasks concerning accidental pollution of transboundary inland waters. Where countries act within such institutions, they should make every effort to take the provisions of this Code into account.

3. The formal character, functions and geographical and substantive scope of existing commissions should, where necessary, be broadened to deal with protection of transboundary inland waters against accidental pollution and to cope with such incidents in the best possible way. Existing national and intergovernmental structures and legal provisions should be fully taken into account, as well as hydrological, environmental, economic and other relevant conditions. Joint commissions should be used to facilitate co-operation and communication between the national authorities concerned, in particular between designated points of contact of participating countries.

VI. EXCHANGE OF INFORMATION

1. Riparian countries should, in accordance with the provisions of this Code:

(a) Exchange information on their legislative and administrative measures as well as their policies, scientific activities and technical measures to prevent, control and reduce accidental pollution of transboundary inland waters and to mitigate and contain damage from such pollution with a view to harmonizing such measures;

(b) Provide for the exchange of information on:

    (i) Incidents, measures and plans at the national level affecting other countries;

    (ii) Objectives and standards, as well as programmes for monitoring, planning, research and development including their implementation and surveillance;

    (iii) Data regarding the control of accidental pollution of transboundary inland waters.

2. For purposes of expeditious communications between the countries concerned, each country should designate a national governmental authority as point of contact competent to perform the administrative functions related to the exchange of information. Countries should inform each other of these authorities and of any changes in their functions.

3. In order to facilitate and expedite the exchange of information pertinent to the implementation of their relevant agreements or arrangements, countries concerned should consider the possibility of establishing communication links between the regional and/or local authorities of adjacent areas, integrated in and co-ordinated with any intergovernmental system of information exchange.

4. Riparian countries should exchange information regarding the authorization of planned activities involving a significant risk of accidental pollution of transboundary inland waters.

5. Countries exchanging information in accordance with this Code should establish internal procedures for the receipt, handling and protection of confidential and proprietary information received from other countries.

VII. ACCESS TO PROCEEDINGS

1. In order to promote informed decision-making by central, regional or local authorities in proceedings concerning accidental pollution of transboundary inland waters, countries should facilitate participation of the public likely to be affected in hearings and preliminary inquiries and the making of objections in respect of proposed decisions, as well as recourse to and standing in administrative and judicial proceedings.

2. Countries of incident should take all appropriate measures to provide physical and legal persons exposed to a significant risk of accidental pollution of transboundary inland waters with sufficient information to enable them to exercise the rights accorded to them by national law in accordance with the objectives of this Code.

3. Countries should endeavour, in accordance with their legal systems and, where appropriate, on the basis of mutual agreements, to provide physical and legal persons in other countries, who have been or may be adversely affected by accidental pollution of transboundary inland waters, with equivalent access to and treatment in the same administrative and judicial proceedings, and make available to them the same

remedies as are available to persons within their own jurisdiction who have been or may be similarly affected.

4. Where the law of a country of incident permits a public authority competent to safeguard general environmental interests, to participate in administrative or judicial proceedings, the country of incident should consider the possibility of providing equivalent public authorities of the exposed country with access to such proceedings.

5. Where, during the authorization procedure referred to in section IX, there are reasonable grounds to believe that pollution of transboundary inland waters within the territory of a country other than the authorizing country resulting from incidents relating to an activity subject to authorization cannot be reasonably excluded, the authorizing country should inform the exposed country about the activity as soon as it has sufficient information on the possible effect of the activity, and not later than when informing its own nationals.

6. As to possibilities of appropriate access to proceedings by the exposed countries as well as by physical and legal persons, countries should take duly into account environmental impact assessment (EIA) procedures in a transboundary context which will provide, *inter alia*, for risk assessment and reduction of risk of accidents with transboundary impacts thus preventing accidental pollution.

7. If necessary, both the authorizing and the exposed country should without undue delay enter into consultations and negotiations in order to verify and determine the risk and amount of accidental pollution of transboundary inland waters, aiming at arriving at an arrangement with regard to the necessary adjustments and modifications of planned activities, safety measures or off-site and on-site contingency plans that would give the exposed country reasonable satisfaction.

8. Where an installation involved in activities subject to authorization is owned, or activities subject to authorization are performed, by a person not under the jurisdiction of the authorizing country, a representative of that person within the jurisdiction of the authorizing country should be duly empowered

9

to act on that person's behalf and account. This representative should also be in a position to meet any financial obligations that may arise from such activities or installations.

VIII. ECONOMIC INSTRUMENTS

1.   Countries should consider all possible economic measures which could promote the prevention, control and reduction of accidental pollution of transboundary inland waters, as well as suitable remedial measures to cope with critical situations caused by such pollution.   In the formulation and application of economic instruments for this purpose, attention should be paid, in particular, to:

(a) Their optimal combination with existing patterns of legal, administrative and technical instruments;

(b) Their consistency with prevailing economic principles; and

(c) Anticipated changes of water-use practices owing to the measures applied.

2.   Economic including fiscal instruments should be employed, where appropriate and possible, in order to:

(a) Induce   operators   to   anticipate   the   environmental consequences of their activities regarding transboundary inland waters and to adopt the necessary safety regulations and standards;

(b) Encourage operators to substitute hazardous substances in their   production   processes   by   non-hazardous   or   less hazardous substances;

(c) Promote the development, application and exchange of information on new technologies and equipment reducing the risk of accidental pollution of transboundary inland waters.

3.   Adequate financial and other resources should be made available, in accordance with national law and practice, for administrative tasks in relation to accidental pollution of transboundary inland waters.

IX. REGULATORY INSTRUMENTS

1. Countries should, by all appropriate measures:

(a) Provide criteria and procedures forming the basis for the authorization of hazardous activities, whether governmental or undertaken by physical or legal persons, that are likely to lead to accidental pollution of transboundary inland waters;

(b) Ensure that such activities be subject to authorization according to the terms and conditions specified in annex C.

2. The activities subject to authorization should comprise those which are classified as hazardous by the authorizing country, or which are connected with the use of hazardous substances as laid down by the authorizing country.

3. Countries should ensure that applications for authorization contain an assessment of the anticipated impact on the environment as specified in annex C. On the basis of a bilateral or multilateral agreement an environmental impact assessment (EIA) should also be undertaken if so requested by an exposed country that has reasonable grounds to believe that the transboundary inland waters within its territory could be affected by an activity planned in the other country in case of incident; it is necessary that such a request be accompanied by the stated reasons and sufficient evidence.

4. Criteria and procedures for determining whether an activity is subject to an EIA should be defined clearly by legislation, regulation, or other means, so that activities subject to authorization can be identified quickly and accurately, and an EIA can be undertaken as the activity is being planned. Any authorization procedure should contain a mechanism for ensuring that the results of EIA are adequately taken into account in the decision-making process. The way in which the findings are taken into account should be documented as appropriate.

5. Any authorization should specify, directly or by referring to the applicable legislative or administrative measures, the obligations imposed on the operator such as those laid down in annex C. Operators should also be informed about the

competent governmental authorities designated as points of contact for issuing and receiving notifications in accordance with paragraph 2 of section VI.

6. Countries should keep registers and other records of authorizations granted for hazardous activities. The competent authority should be in a position to *(a)* survey the installations regularly in order to ensure that the conditions under which the authorization was issued are being met, and *(b)* to enforce the terms of the authorization and, if necessary, to suspend or revoke it if the terms and conditions laid down therein are not met.

7. Hazardous activities should not be authorized unless it is established that *(a)* the planned activities and substances involved therein are subject to adequate safety measures to minimize the risk of accidental pollution of transboundary inland waters; and/or *(b)* in case of accidental pollution, significant adverse effects on the aquatic environment of another country could not be avoided by compliance with the conditions in the authorization.

X. RISK AND VULNERABILITY ASSESSMENTS

1. Countries should ensure, in accordance with their legal systems, that an analysis and assessment of the risks of accidental pollution of transboundary inland waters is undertaken in the course of the authorization procedure referred to in section IX and is subsequently reviewed when circumstances so require. Such risk assessment should include procedures to identify and assess hazardous activities and substances, taking into account the hazard identification techniques contained in annex D.

2. The objectives of risk assessments should be the identification of the nature and scale of potential accidental releases of hazardous substances into the aquatic environment, laying down the basis for contingency plans, the identification of the type, likelihood and broad consequences of major accidents and disasters that might occur. To this end countries should ensure the establishment, *inter alia*, of inventories as specified in annex D.

3. Countries having carried out risk assessments should inform other countries concerned, regularly and/or when circumstances so require, of the results of such assessments, so as to enable these countries to take the necessary preventive and remedial measures.

4. Countries concerned should co-ordinate their assessments of the risk of accidental pollution of transboundary inland waters by using comparable methods, data and criteria and, where appropriate, harmonize the criteria of such assessments. Where appropriate, joint assessment should be envisaged which would allow for common conclusions with respect to mutual interests.

5. Countries should carry out vulnerability assessments of transboundary inland waters with a view to identifying sensitive areas with regard to their ecological situation with particular emphasis on their water resources. Other countries concerned should be notified of these areas.

6. Land-use planning and proper allocation of water resources should be given priority as an effective means to prevent accidental pollution of transboundary inland waters. To this end, countries should ensure that hazardous activities or substances likely to cause such pollution should be excluded from sensitive or protected areas and adequate buffer zones should be established between hazardous installations and sensitive or protected transboundary inland waters. Increased attention should be paid to the control of abandoned sites of hazardous waste disposal and to closed facilities of hazardous activities, with a view to minimizing the risk of accidental pollution.

XI. CONTINGENCY PLANS

1. Countries authorizing hazardous activities should ensure the development and, whenever necessary, application of contingency plans at all levels to prevent, control and reduce accidental pollution of transboundary inland waters by using all available resources in the most efficient way.

2. Operators should be required to establish on-site contingency plans in accordance with annex E, and to assess regularly the effectiveness of such plans.

3.   Countries should elaborate and adopt appropriate off-site contingency plans in accordance with annex E.   Such off-site contingency plans should be drawn up at the national, regional and/or local level and should be compatible with those to be established by operators.   On-site and off-site contingency plans should be interlocked to ensure that they provide a comprehensive and effective response to incidents.

4.   Countries concerned should endeavour to co-ordinate their national contingency plans relating to transboundary inland waters, to harmonize them as well as the criteria on which the contingency plans are based or, where appropriate, to draw up joint contingency plans.

XII. EARLY WARNING AND ALARM SYSTEMS

1.   Countries should set up and operate efficient warning and alarm systems with the aim of obtaining and transmitting reliable information needed to counteract accidental pollution of transboundary inland waters.   Warning and alarm systems should consist of main communication centres which, on the basis of a national reporting system, should ensure the speediest possible transmission of data and forecasts following previously determined patterns.   These warning and alarm systems should permit early undertaking of corrective and protective measures, containment of damage and reduction of risks.   To this effect, countries should seek to establish common communication systems including mutually agreed codes for emergency warning and response, and compatible data-transmission and treatment systems.

2.   Countries concerned should make known to each other their competent points of contact and communication centres responsible for the timely issuing, receipt and transmission of the respective notifications and information, and ensure the efficiency of these centres.   The countries concerned should promptly inform each other of any changes that may occur in the information referred to above.

3. Countries concerned should at regular intervals test and review the efficacy of warning and alarm systems, and ensure regular training of the personnel involved in warning and alarm operations. Where appropriate, the countries concerned should perform such tests, reviews and training jointly.

XIII. NOTIFICATION OF INCIDENTS

1. Countries should ensure that in an incident or in an imminent threat of accidental pollution of transboundary inland waters, operators comply with the contingency plans referred to in section XI.

2. In an incident entailing the risk of accidental pollution of transboundary inland waters in the territory of another country, the country of incident should forthwith notify all exposed countries and provide additional information in accordance with annex F, taking into account the information furnished by the operator.

3. Countries should in due time notify all exposed countries of any significant change of circumstances likely to cause or aggravate accidental pollution of transboundary inland waters in the territories of exposed countries.

4. Any warning, notification of emergency situations or transmittal of additional information among the countries concerned should be made through the designated points of contact referred to in paragraph 2 of section VI or, if the urgency requires, through other competent authorities that may be expected to ensure an efficient treatment of the information.

XIV. DAMAGE CONTAINMENT AND REHABILITATION

1. Countries concerned should ensure that operators make use under their control of the most efficient practices to contain and abate accidental pollution of transboundary inland waters, by appropriate treatment, collection, recovery, storage and/or safe disposal of pollutants and polluted material, in particular by taking the measures specified in annex G. In cases where operators take no action or insufficient action, or in other cases where it is deemed necessary, countries should, where

appropriate, have necessary measures carried out at operators' own expense and risk.

2. Exposed countries should communicate to the country of incident any information and observation relating to the assessment of damage and development of the situation concerning transboundary inland waters affected by accidental pollution in areas under their jurisdiction, in order to enable the country of incident to take the necessary measures to abate and/or contain such pollution at source.

3. For the purpose of effective co-ordination and harmonization of contingency measures, the countries concerned should convene committees consisting of representatives of competent authorities involved. Where and when appropriate, the operator, other persons involved such as safety officers and physical or legal persons affected by the incident could be given an opportunity to participate in these committees.

4. To facilitate co-operation for this purpose, riparian countries should, where appropriate, agree on bilateral or multilateral arrangements for rendering mutual assistance in such events; they should, in particular, consider the possibility to include the rendering of such assistance in joint contingency plans. Such arrangements should contain specific provisions relating to mutual assistance such as direction, control, co-ordination and supervision of assistance; local facilities and services to be rendered by the requesting country, including the reduction or waiver of border-crossing formalities; reimbursement for assistance services; the necessary privileges, immunities and facilities to be accorded by the requesting country; arrangements for holding harmless, indemnifying and/or compensating the assisting country or its personnel as well as transit through third countries, where necessary.

5. Countries should, within the limits of their capabilities, identify and notify other countries about experts, equipment and materials which can be made available for the provision of assistance to countries concerned in pollution incidents, as well as about the financial and other terms under which such assistance can be provided.

6. Countries receiving a request for assistance should promptly inform the requesting country whether they are in a position to render the assistance required, and indicate the scope and terms of the assistance available.

XV. DAMAGE ASSESSMENT AND COMPENSATION

1. Countries should seek to ensure in their national legislation prompt and adequate compensation in respect of damage caused by accidental pollution of transboundary inland waters according to the provisions of this Code.

2. When an accidental pollution of transboundary inland waters occurs, the countries concerned should at the expense of the polluter take all necessary steps to assess the actual and potential damage, as provided for in annex H. Countries concerned should co-operate, as far as practicable, to assist each other in damage assessment, and with a view to harmonizing the methods, criteria and procedures for such assessment.

3. In accordance with the polluter-pays principle referred to in paragraph 3 of section II, countries should co-operate in the implementation and further development of appropriate rules and practices to ensure redress for the victims of accidental pollution of transboundary inland waters and necessary rehabilitation measures. Countries should enter into or accelerate discussions for the elaboration of liability systems including the establishment of funds or insurance systems for pollution damage.

4. In order to ensure prompt and adequate compensation in respect of all damage caused by accidental pollution of transboundary inland waters, countries should in accordance with their national legal system provide for the identification of the physical or legal person or persons liable for damage resulting from hazardous activities. Unless otherwise provided, the operator should be considered liable; and where more than one organization or person is liable, such liability should be joint and several. Countries should ensure that recourse is available in accordance with their legal systems for compensation.

5. Countries should provide strict liability for pollution damage caused by accidents involving hazardous activities bearing in

mind exonerating circumstances. The organization or person liable for damage should be held to incur liability upon proof that the damage was caused by an accident in the installation for which it/he is responsible.

6. For cases of pollution of transboundary inland waters, where the incident from which the damage resulted cannot be identified, and in order to facilitate the payment of compensation to persons who have suffered damage caused by accidental pollution of transboundary inland waters, countries should, *inter alia*, consider the establishment of compensation funds. Such funds might be established to deal with cases in which damage remains wholly or partly uncompensated.

7. Countries of incident should ensure that any person who has suffered damage resulting from accidental pollution or is exposed to a significant risk of accidental pollution of transboundary inland waters, receive treatment at least equivalent to that afforded in the country of incident in comparable domestic circumstances, to persons of equivalent condition or status.

XVI. POST-ACCIDENT SURVEILLANCE

1. After any incident resulting in accidental pollution of transboundary inland waters, the countries concerned should, through their competent authorities at all levels, survey the consequences for the environment, including pollutant concentrations, persistence and distribution in the aquatic environment by means of monitoring, survey and research measures. Countries should ensure that adequate institutional arrangements are made at the appropriate level for the purpose of reporting on measures taken, on results achieved and, if the case arises, on difficulties encountered in the implementation and application of provisions contained in relevant international agreements or national legislative and administrative measures including contingency plans.

2. Countries should draw up reports based on such information and make them available to other countries concerned. The countries concerned should assist each other in the interpretation and assessment of such reports, in particular in the assessment of the efficiency of rehabilitation measures.

3. The experience gained in coping with accidental pollution incidents should be used to the fullest extent possible as feedback for the progressive development and application of preventive measures and for the improvement of contingency plans. The countries concerned should co-operate in drawing conclusions from such experience.

ANNEX A

MATTERS TO BE REGULATED

National legislative and administrative measures for the prevention, control and reduction of accidental pollution of transboundary inland waters should provide, in particular, for:

(a) Safety objectives, safety standards and safety measures;

(b) Hazard identification for activities and substances which require special preventive measures and are subject to authorization as well as risk assessment;

(c) Authorization procedures for activities which because of their hazardous nature or because of the use of hazardous substances may result in accidental pollution of transboundary inland waters;

(d) Inventories of accidents and natural disasters relating to transboundary inland waters;

(e) Inventories of sensitive areas, i.e. areas which are particularly vulnerable to pollution of transboundary inland waters;

(f) Off-site contingency planning for hazardous activities, including public information requirements;

(g) On-site contingency plans to be established by operators;

(h) Long-term water management plans taking accidental pollution aspects into account as well as land-use plans regulating the siting of hazardous activities and of new developments near existing hazardous activities;

(i) Containment and rehabilitation programmes for accidental pollution incidents;

(j) Liability and compensation for damage caused by accidental pollution of transboundary inland waters;

(k) Appropriate regulatory powers for competent administrative authorities, including pre-accident and post-accident monitoring, unimpeded access to, as well as inspection and control of hazardous activities;

(l) Adequate sanctions for non-compliance;

(m) Economic incentives and disincentives;

(n) Protection of confidential and proprietary data;

(o) Mutual assistance in accidental pollution incidents;

(p) Support for participation in relevant international institutions and programmes.

ANNEX B

FUNCTIONS OF INTERNATIONAL INSTITUTIONS FOR TRANSBOUNDARY INLAND WATERS

Joint commissions and other co-operation bodies dealing with transboundary inland waters should be entrusted with the function, *inter alia*:

(a) To serve as advisory and negotiating body in all matters regarding accidental pollution of transboundary inland waters;

(b) To develop water protection objectives and standards as well as joint arrangements, control programmes, and common methodologies to deal with accidental pollution of transboundary inland waters;

(c) To monitor and assess data relating to accidental pollution as well as to survey the state of transboundary inland waters and to control the effectiveness of measures implemented as a basis for new measures;

(d) To prepare on the basis of results obtained from monitoring programmes inventories of transboundary inland waters sensitive to accidental pollution, as well as inventories of potential sources of accidental pollution;

(e) To arrange for and carry out relevant research work in order to determine the nature, significance and origin of accidental pollution of transboundary inland waters;

(f) To develop, establish and operate early detection and warning systems;

(g) To examine the possibilities for further measures and co-operation including improved exchange of information on topical issues in preventing and mitigating accidental pollution including experience gained in the application and operation of technology and results of research in this field;

(h) To initiate necessary measures aimed at harmonizing or making compatible contingency plans and legislation on matters covered by this Code;

(i) To develop joint or co-ordinated monitoring programmes and off-site contingency plans;

(j) To promote co-operation between the competent local authorities of adjacent frontier regions for the prevention and control of accidental pollution of transboundary inland waters, and to facilitate the participation and representation of such authorities in international co-operative arrangements;

(k) To prepare inventories of technical facilities available to the countries concerned, to prevent, control and reduce accidental pollution and to promote the international compatibility of such facilities;

(l) To arrange for mutual assistance upon request, and to make available to requesting countries facilities for preventing and controlling accidental pollution and for rehabilitating polluted transboundary inland waters;

(m) To monitor, as far as possible, the effectiveness and compatibility of control measures implemented at the national level and to evaluate the extent to which the objectives of relevant agreements are met;

(n) To arrange for joint manoeuvres and equipment tests and exercises of competent services and facilities such as civil protection and rescue units, fire and oil brigades;

(o) To take steps as required for the identification of the source or origin of accidental pollution of transboundary inland waters;

(p) To ensure liaison with other international institutions concerned and to seek advice from experts and scientific institutes, if necessary;

(q) To prepare and publish regular reports on work accomplished and information supplied;

(r) To develop common principles such as a set of guidelines for the use of economic instruments at the national level in order to promote the application of safety measures in hazardous activities;

(s) To establish specific codes of good practice on prevention and mitigation of accidental pollution for transboundary inland waters.

ANNEX C

TERMS AND CONDITIONS OF ADMINISTRATIVE AUTHORIZATION

1. The information to be furnished by an applicant for authorization of hazardous activities should contain the following elements, including those resulting from an environmental impact assessment (EIA) as appropriate:

(a) A description of the proposed hazardous activities and the substances to be used as well as of management of waste generated;

(b) An indication of the authorities required to act upon the documentation and of the nature of the decision;

(c) A description of potential sources and causes of incidents in connection with the proposed activities;

(d) A description of the conditions of the water resources potentially affected by incidents in connection with the proposed activities, including specific information necessary for identifying and assessing the adverse effects of such incidents;

(e) A description of reasonable main alternatives, as appropriate, including the no-action alternative;

(f) An assessment of the potential adverse impacts on transboundary inland waters likely to result from incidents in connection with the proposed activities and main alternatives, as well as the socio-economic consequences of environmental change owing to such activities or alternatives, including direct, indirect, cumulative, short-term and long-term, secondary and synergetic effects;

(g) Relevant environmental data used and an explanation of predictive methods and assumptions made in the course of the assessment;

(h) Information about contingency procedures laid down for dealing with an accident occurring at the site;

(i) An identification and description of measures available to prevent incidents and to mitigate adverse impacts on transboundary inland waters of the proposed activities and alternatives and an assessment of those measures as well as information on compliance with relevant safety standards;

(j) An outline of monitoring programmes, management tools and mitigation measures for minimizing water-resources degradation;

(k) An indication of whether the aquatic environment of any other countries may be affected by the proposed activities or alternatives;

(l) An indication of uncertainties encountered in compiling the required information;

(m) A non-technical summary including appropriate visual presentation (maps, graphs, etc.).

2. The obligations imposed on an operator, to be included in the authorization, should comprise among others the following, as appropriate:

(a) To comply with safety standards and to set up reliable warning systems for early detection of any impending or probable accidental pollution of transboundary inland waters;

(b) To monitor all phases of the hazardous activity;

(c) To provide special equipment necessary for preventing accidental pollution or for limiting the detrimental effects of such pollution including transboundary pollution;

(d) To establish an on-site contingency plan;

(e) To designate an appropriate and qualified person as "safety officer" responsible for providing the appropriate information, implementing safety measures, notifying and receiving information, and checking on-site contingency plans;

(f) To take preventive measures and to maintain preventive arrangements, e.g. by regular inspections;

(g) To permit inspection and surveys by governmental authorities on site and off site at regular and random intervals in order to ensure that the conditions under which the authorization was issued are being met;

(h) To provide access for the competent authorities in case of an incident;

(i) To assess the effects of the activity on transboundary inland waters and in case of an unexpected increase of risks as compared to the original conditions for the authorization, to report on these to the competent authority in accordance with established procedures;

(j) To enter an insurance or any other equivalent means to cover risks which are to be insured according to the law of that country in respect of damage to third parties arising from accidental pollution of transboundary inland waters.

3. The safety measures imposed on an operator, to be included in the authorization, should comprise, among others, the following as appropriate:

(a) Adequate design and construction of installations taking into account foreseeable natural circumstances;

(b) Adequate instrumentation such as protective devices, safety and prevention equipment, and alarm systems;

(c) Development and application of operating procedures for safety installations;

(d) Continuous supervision and periodic inspection of safety installations;

(e) Permanent monitoring of hazardous activities;

(f) Adequate manning of the installations involved in hazardous activities;

(g) Suitable qualifications and experience of persons engaged in hazardous activities, taking into account all existing standards and the best available techniques;

(h) Adequate training programmes, including training on a continuing basis, particularly as regards safety and environmental matters;

(i) Application of relevant national and international rules, standards and recommended practices and procedures as regards occupational safety during all phases of activities.

ANNEX D

HAZARD IDENTIFICATION TECHNIQUES

Hazardous activities likely to cause accidental pollution of transboundary inland waters should be identified by means of appropriate techniques and procedures such as:

(a) Description of the production unit where hazardous substances are handled, including the amount and characteristics of these substances;

(b) Review of hazardous substances present on the site and/or used in the production process regarding their physical and chemical properties and their characteristics concerning toxicology and ecotoxicology, bio-accumulativity and persistence, flammability and explosion, reactivity to common ambient media such as water and air as well as potential ways in which the accidental release of such substances from their normal containment may result in pollution of the transboundary inland waters;

(c) Design checking concerning process, operations, equipment and instrumentation, including characteristics of the material for construction and installation involved;

(d) Description and analysis of the existing or planned safety measures compared to safety standards as well as evaluation of damages to be expected in case of any incident occurring despite safety measures applied;

(e) Description of substantial hazard scenarios owing to accidental pollution caused by man-made accidents and natural disasters including their potential impact on transboundary inland waters, giving due consideration to the existing or planned safety measures;

(f) Evaluation of accidental pollution hazards resulting from operational errors as well as of breakdown of safety devices, using appropriate analysis techniques, such as "fault-tree" or "event-tree" techniques concentrating on sensitive sectors of hazardous activities;

(g) Review of process stability under departures from normal conditions, in order to identify potential hazards and to ensure that operating procedures are inherently safe so that the consequences of possible errors are minimized as far as possible;

(h) Qualitative failure studies to identify accidental pollution hazard due to malfunctioning of certain operations during start-up and shut-down phases or during loading or unloading;

(i) Inventories and analyses of past incidents of accidental pollution drawn up for specific production sectors and according to causes either internal or external, direct or indirect;

(j) Application of safety audits and quality assurance programmes during construction, commissioning, operation and maintenance;

(k) Installation layout survey, to examine existence of buffer zones, of safe roads without impediment to freedom of movement of traffic, and adequate spacing of hazardous installations;

(l) Evaluation of the remaining risk; conclusions for additional safety measures to be included in relevant contingency plans;

(m) Check-lists allowing immediate assessment and warning on serious danger for accidental pollution of transboundary inland waters.

ANNEX E

CONTINGENCY PLANS

1. On-site contingency plans to be established by operators, should provide appropriate measures to prevent and control accidents, to limit and mitigate impacts on transboundary inland waters, to provide persons working on the site with the necessary information, training and equipment, and, in particular, should include arrangements for:

(a) The immediate raising of an alarm in the area of operations, including rapid warning of the authority or authorities designated for that purpose and for transmitting information related to any significant change in risk of a hazardous activity;

(b) An up-to-date list of persons to be alerted and informed, together with the speediest means and necessary information available for making contact with them;

(c) A continuous flow of full information to the authority or authorities designated for that purpose, relating to particulars of the contingency, measures already taken and further action required;

(d) Unimpeded access to the site for the competent authorities and authorized experts;

(e) Compatibility and co-ordination with off-site contingency plans drawn up by the competent authorities, and mutual assistance among operators;

(f) Identification of the nature and quantity of hazardous substances present on the site, as well as potential ways in which the accidental release of such substances from their normal containment may result in pollution of the transboundary inland waters;

(g) Identification of the designated safety officer, and an inventory of means available to him to prevent, control and reduce accidental pollution of transboundary inland waters and of any special safety arrangements aimed at preventing potentially hazardous deviations from normal operations,

including an alarm system and measures to limit the consequences of an incident;

(h) Primary preventive measures (proper design, construction, operation, maintenance, inspection and periodic exercises of the safety installations);

(i) Emergency measures to be taken under the direction of the safety officer, in particular for the protection of human life;

(j) Technical measures for containment of the flow of hazardous substances, extinguishing of fires, safe removal and disposal of polluting substances and polluted materials;

(k) Identification of the transport of dangerous substances in various media — air, surface water, ground water, soil — as well as in sewage systems, paying due attention to sampling sites, parameters to be measured and analytical methods to be applied, which will serve as bases for deciding on emergency and follow-up measures as well as for assessing damage.

2. Off-site contingency plans to be established by competent authorities should include, in particular:

(a) Pre-determined procedures according to the various categories of incidents, aimed at preventing, controlling and reducing accidental pollution of transboundary inland waters, and designation of the competent authorities;

(b) A description of the material and equipment required for emergency measures;

(c) An indication of the competent authorities and available facilities for physical-chemical treatment, containment, removal, storage and/or disposal of hazardous substances and polluted materials, as well as for rehabilitation measures;

(d) A procedure under which the competent authority may intervene whenever necessary, either by giving directions to the safety officer or by undertaking direct action;

(e) Supervision of hazardous activities at all times during emergencies;

(f) Ready availability, at strategically placed centres and as required by the location of hazardous activities, of the necessary trained personnel, equipment and materials necessary for prevention, control and reduction of accidental pollution of transboundary inland waters;

(g) Procedures and channels of public information on emergencies and emergency measures;

(h) Expeditious communication on emergencies with the competent authorities, including the authorities of other countries concerned, and designation of a point of contact responsible for communication with other countries concerned;

(i) Arrangements for consultations of the competent authorities of the countries concerned regarding the terms and conditions of authorizations for hazardous activities;

(j) Exchange of information between the countries concerned on the on-site contingency plans established by operators;

(k) Exchange of information between the countries concerned on the availability of personnel, equipment and materials necessary for the prevention, control and reduction of accidental pollution of transboundary inland waters;

(l) A procedure under which the competent authorities of any exposed country other than the authorizing country may have access, with the latter's consent, to the site of the incident;

(m) Arrangements for alternative water supply in case of accidental pollution of transboundary inland waters.

3. Off-site contingency plans should take into account, in particular:

(a) The on-site contingency plans established by operators, and their capacity to implement these plans, as well as other relevant legal and administrative requirements;

(b) The ecological vulnerability and the actual use of water resources including transboundary waters in the areas potentially affected by pollution incidents;

(c) The probability, nature and consequences of potential incidents, including the amount of damage, the risk of explosions or of release of hazardous substances into transboundary inland waters, and the influence of pollutants on food chains or transport cycles through the aquatic environment;

(d) The characteristics of hazardous substances involved, in particular their toxic, persistent or bio-accumulative nature;

(e) The expected duration of the emergency situation.

ANNEX F

NOTIFICATION AND INFORMATION ON INCIDENTS

The information to be provided by the country of incidence to the exposed country(ies) in case of an incident or imminent threat of accidental pollution of transboundary inland waters should comprise:

(a) The time, location, nature and quantitative dimensions of the incident;

(b) The event which is most likely to be the origin of accidental pollution as well as the activity or facility involved;

(c) The media polluted, including their location and characteristics;

(d) Any hazardous substances released, including their nature, composition (by chemical formulae or other appropriate identification), quantity, effects on human health and on the aquatic environment, the extent of their distribution in transboundary inland waters and adjacent land as a result of the incident, and the results of any monitoring relevant to the release and behaviour of such substances;

(e) The predicted behaviour over time of the pollutants released and the possibilities and mechanisms of attenuation of the pollution;

(f) Means of public information as well as forecasting systems;

(g) The on-site and off-site contingency measures taken or planned concerning mitigation, containment and control of accidental pollution, and other emergency measures;

(h) Foreseeable transboundary consequences of the incident;

(i) Any other information which might be useful for the effective prevention or abatement of accidental pollution of transboundary inland waters, including information on current and forecast meteorological, hydrological and hydrogeological conditions as may be necessary for

forecasting potential effects of the pollutants on the aquatic environment in other countries concerned;

(j) Continuous follow-up information, as appropriate, regarding the subsequent evolution of the emergency situation.

ANNEX G

REHABILITATION METHODS AND TECHNIQUES

Appropriate damage containment and rehabilitation methods and techniques, depending on the media polluted and the type of pollution, should be effectively applied, if appropriate, by means of mobile installation including *inter alia*:

(a) Physical detoxification, including techniques of thermal destruction, incineration, filtration;

(b) Biological and chemical treatment processes, including aerobic and anaerobic treatment, neutralization, chemical precipitation, reduction/oxidation processes, *in-situ* enhanced natural biodegradation;

(c) Phase-separated techniques, including interceptor trenches and wells;

(d) Vapour-phase organic chemical techniques, including positive and negative pressure systems for vapour mitigation, venting to atmosphere, adsorption/removal of organics;

(e) Dredging operations and safe treatment and/or disposal of dredged material;

(f) Washing out of river beds and flushing of sensitive areas with clean and appropriately drained water and drainage of polluted soil together with appropriate treatment and discharge of the purified wash-water;

(g) Removal of sensitive aquatic species and transfer to unpolluted aquatic ecosystems for their reimplementation and restocking;

(h) Temporary impounding of the polluted water body;

(i) Diversion to preconstructed reservoirs, construction of interceptor trenches, provisional diversion to treatment sites;

(j) Pumping operations to remove polluted bottom sediments and/or floating hazardous substances.

ANNEX H

DAMAGE ASSESSMENT

The physical and monetary assessment of damage attributed to accidental pollution of transboundary inland waters should contain the following elements:

(a) Review of background data on the pollutants released;

(b) Analysis of soils, hydrological and environmental conditions that affect the release and spreading of pollution;

(c) Evaluation regarding the movement of pollutants in terms of concentration, time, place, environmental media and chemical/biochemical changes in the plume with time;

(d) Examination of affected transboundary inland waters and related ecosystems, as well as of adjacent protection zones for drinking-water abstraction, ground-water recharge areas and other sensitive water bodies that could be damaged;

(e) Evaluation of impacts on the use of transboundary inland waters particularly for domestic sector, agriculture, industry and recreation;

(f) Examination of possible interaction of pollutants;

(g) Monitoring and analysis of water quality and of sediments in terms of pollutant concentrations and load;

(h) Ecotoxicological surveys including biomonitoring analysis and analysis of microphytes;

(i) Evaluation of damage caused by post-accident measures, including containment and rehabilitation measures;

(j) Evaluation of expenditures for monitoring and rehabilitation operations as well as for action designed to prevent the spread of accidental pollution of transboundary inland waters, minimize damage and protect people and the environment against deleterious effects.